Fairy Tale Creatures
Dwarfs

by Sophie Geister-Jones

www.focusreaders.com

Copyright © 2022 by Focus Readers®, Lake Elmo, MN 55042. All rights reserved. No part of this book may be reproduced or utilized in any form or by any means without written permission from the publisher.

Focus Readers is distributed by North Star Editions:
sales@northstareditions.com | 888-417-0195

Produced for Focus Readers by Red Line Editorial.

Photographs ©: Shutterstock Images, cover, 1, 4, 7, 11, 12, 14, 17, 18, 20–21, 22, 25, 27, 29; The Picture Art Collection/Alamy, 8

Library of Congress Cataloging-in-Publication Data
Names: Geister-Jones, Sophie, author.
Title: Dwarfs : fairy tale creatures / Sophie Geister-Jones.
Description: Lake Elmo, MN : Focus Readers, [2022] | Series: Fairy tale creatures | Includes index. | Audience: Grades 2-3
Identifiers: LCCN 2021006315 (print) | LCCN 2021006316 (ebook) | ISBN 9781637390016 (hardcover) | ISBN 9781637390085 (paperback) | ISBN 9781637390153 (ebook) | ISBN 9781637390214 (pdf)
Subjects: LCSH: Dwarfs (Folklore)--Juvenile literature.
Classification: LCC GR555 .G45 2022 (print) | LCC GR555 (ebook) | DDC 398.21--dc23
LC record available at https://lccn.loc.gov/2021006315
LC ebook record available at https://lccn.loc.gov/2021006316

Printed in the United States of America
Mankato, MN
082021

About the Author

Sophie Geister-Jones lives in Saint Paul, Minnesota. She enjoys reading and watching her friends do puzzles while she eats food.

Table of Contents

CHAPTER 1
Master Smiths 5

CHAPTER 2
Dwarfs of Old 9

CHAPTER 3
Small but Strong 15

STORY SPOTLIGHT
Fierce Fighters 20

CHAPTER 4
Gifts and Gold 23

Focus on Dwarfs • 28
Glossary • 30
To Learn More • 31
Index • 32

Chapter 1

Master Smiths

A **forge** burned deep inside a mountain. Coals shone bright in the fire. A stocky dwarf blew air onto them. The flames roared. The coals grew hotter. Soon they were ready for the dwarf to use.

Tools for shaping metal hang in front of the hot fire of a forge.

The dwarf stuck a long pole into the flames. The pole had a lump of metal at one end. This end turned bright red.

The dwarf removed the hot metal from the fire. He walked carefully to his **anvil**. He hit the metal with a hammer. Slowly, he shaped it into a

Fun Fact

Thor is the **Norse** god of thunder. He has a magic hammer. A dwarf made it for him.

 Hot metal shoots out sparks when it is hit with a hammer.

weapon. He formed a short handle and a large hammerhead. It would be a powerful weapon.

Chapter 2

Dwarfs of Old

Many stories of dwarfs come from **Scandinavia**. Some of these stories are thousands of years old. Many are part of the Edda. The Edda is a collection of stories. They come from Norse **mythology**.

Illustrations in the Edda show many kinds of creatures.

These stories were told out loud for many years. In 1223, people began writing them down.

In many of the stories, dwarfs interact with the gods. Sometimes, they fight. Other times, dwarfs have things the gods need.

For example, dwarfs often built weapons for the gods. One dwarf

Fun Fact

Norse myths say four dwarfs hold up the corners of the sky.

 Dwarfs can create strong chain mail and beautiful jewelry.

made a magic ship. The ship could sail on water or air. When not in use, the ship could fold up. It fit in a pocket.

 Small statues of dwarfs appear all over the city of Wroclaw, Poland.

Dwarfs are also part of the Norse creation story. In this story, the world was made from the body of a giant. Maggots grew in his skull.

They wriggled around in the dirt. The gods changed the maggots into dwarfs. The dwarfs looked similar to humans. But they lived underground or in rocks.

Other **cultures** have their own stories of dwarfs. Some of these dwarfs live underground. Others live in forests.

One **legend** says dwarfs cause the northern lights with their cooking fires.

Chapter 3

Small but Strong

Dwarfs are best known for their short height. They are usually the size of a human child. Some dwarfs have hunched backs that make them even shorter.

In some stories, dwarfs wear helmets and armor.

Dwarfs' bodies are broad and strong. They often have long beards. In many stories, they look like old men. They often wear hats.

In Norse mythology, dwarfs live in their own **realm**. It is a world of darkness. It is almost all underground. Systems of tunnels join everything together. Dwarfs dig mines. There, they search for metals and jewels.

In other stories, dwarfs live in the same world as humans. But they

 Sometimes dwarfs find trolls or other monsters in their tunnels.

still live mostly underground. These dwarfs often make their homes in mountains. They dig tunnels through the rock.

17

 The hammer that dwarfs gave the god Thor was called Mjollnir.

Dwarfs use forges to do metalwork. First, they heat the metal in a fire. Then, they pound the hot metal with a hammer. They shape it into tools or weapons. For example, they often make swords and rings. Many of these objects have magical powers. Dwarfs sometimes give them as gifts to gods.

In one story, dwarfs made a gold boar. It was covered in tiny gold hairs. And it was very shiny. The boar shone so bright that it could turn night into day.

Fun Fact

In some stories, dwarfs can be invisible. In others, they can shape-shift.

STORY SPOTLIGHT

Fierce Fighters

J. R. R. Tolkien wrote several famous **fantasy** novels. His books feature many magical creatures, including dwarfs. The dwarfs in Tolkien's books live deep underground. They have entire cities and kingdoms underneath mountains. They also speak their own language.

Tolkien's dwarfs are stocky and strong. They can carry heavy things. And they can live a long time. Many of them are warriors. Some fight with swords and shields. Others use axes or hammers. Dwarfs also wear helmets and armor.

Tolkien's stories tell of dwarfs fighting huge battles.

Chapter 4

Gifts and Gold

Dwarfs tend to live in groups. They build huge halls and cities. The walls and buildings are made of stone. Many dwarfs love their homes. They will fight bravely to defend them.

Dwarfs' underground kingdoms can have towering buildings.

Dwarfs like shiny things. They fill their halls with gold. They also decorate their homes with jewels.

Dwarfs spend a lot of time at their forges. They can make many beautiful objects. But they have other skills, too.

Some stories say dwarfs are wise. They know many secrets. Sometimes, dwarfs can even see the future.

Gods and humans visit dwarfs to ask for help. The dwarfs often

 Similar to dwarfs, dragons are known for collecting gold.

provide useful gifts or advice. But they may punish people who try to steal from them. Other dwarfs try to avoid humans.

25

In some legends, dwarfs are evil. They steal food. They even kidnap women and children. They drag these people back to their tunnels. In some cases, the humans never return home.

However, most stories say dwarfs are kind and helpful. For example,

Miners sometimes left gifts of food for dwarfs. They hoped the food would keep the dwarfs from getting angry.

 Dwarfs continue to appear in stories today.

some dwarfs help farmers. If animals get lost, dwarfs herd them back to the farm. Dwarfs may also share food with people. They make people's lives easier.

FOCUS ON
Dwarfs

Write your answers on a separate piece of paper.

1. Write a paragraph explaining how dwarfs use their forges.
2. Would you want to live in underground tunnels like a dwarf? Why or why not?
3. Where do dwarfs search for metal and jewels?
   - **A.** in anvils
   - **B.** in mines
   - **C.** in forges
4. Why might people ask a dwarf to tell the future?
   - **A.** The dwarf could warn them about problems they will face.
   - **B.** The dwarf could change what will happen.
   - **C.** The dwarf could make them disappear.

5. What does **novels** mean in this book?

J. R. R. Tolkien wrote several famous fantasy novels. His books feature many magical creatures, including dwarfs.

    A. books that tell true stories
    B. books that tell made-up stories
    C. songs on the radio

6. What does **evil** mean in this book?

In some legends, dwarfs are evil. They steal food. They even kidnap women and children.

    A. not real
    B. kind and helpful
    C. bad or mean

Answer key on page 32.

Glossary

anvil
A large block of metal with a flat top that workers use to shape metal.

cultures
Groups of people and the ways they live, including their customs, beliefs, and laws.

fantasy
Involving magic or mythical creatures.

forge
A very hot fire used for melting and shaping metal.

legend
A well-known story from the past. Some legends are based on facts, but not all legends are true.

mythology
A culture's traditional stories that explain the world in some way.

Norse
Related to Norway or other parts of Scandinavia.

realm
A kingdom or world.

Scandinavia
An area in northern Europe that includes the countries of Norway, Sweden, and Denmark. Finland and Iceland may also be included.

To Learn More

BOOKS

Buckey, A. W. *Norse Gods, Heroes, and Mythology*. Minneapolis: Abdo Publishing, 2019.

Crossley-Holland, Kevin. *Norse Myths: Tales of Odin, Thor, and Loki*. Somerville, MA: Candlewick Press, 2017.

Sautter, A. J. *Discover Gnomes, Halflings, and Other Wondrous Fantasy Beings*. Mankato, MN: Capstone Press, 2018.

NOTE TO EDUCATORS

Visit **www.focusreaders.com** to find lesson plans, activities, links, and other resources related to this title.

Index

F
forge, 5, 18, 24

G
gods, 6, 10, 13, 19, 24

J
jewels, 16, 24

M
metal, 6, 16, 18
mines, 16, 26
mountains, 5, 17, 20

S
Scandinavia, 9
swords, 18, 20

T
Tolkien, J. R. R., 20
tunnels, 16–17, 26

U
underground, 13, 16–17, 20

W
weapons, 7, 10, 18

Answer Key: 1. Answers will vary; **2.** Answers will vary; **3.** B; **4.** A; **5.** B; **6.** C